The Idle Lighthouse

A collection of poetry

Written by Karalyn Elyse
Illustrated by Carys Rae

For the quietly audacious dreamers

for those who are waiting for a breakthrough.

Introduction

Here in your hands is something that I didn't think was possible a little over two years ago. As I am writing this, I am overjoyed and astounded by the sheer magic of this experience. I began writing poetry as an outlet as I struggled with depression, anxiety, and loneliness. The poems I wrote during that period of time are stored away; perhaps one day they will see the light, but for now they will stay in my poetry notebook on my shelf.

No, this collection is the aftermath. The beautiful breakthrough that was given to me, undeservedly so, which led to dreaming again. It led to whimsy and curiosity and it translated to the poems in this collection.

The Idle Lighthouse is a place that I find my mind wandering to in daydreams. It resides by cliffs where mer-people and fae folk gather. It houses many doors that lead to adventure. Simply put, The Idle Lighthouse is possibility incarnate.

My hope is that as you read these, your mind feels a spark. A spark of wonder. A spark of yearning. A spark, that may one day turn into a flame that will fuel your soul for adventure.

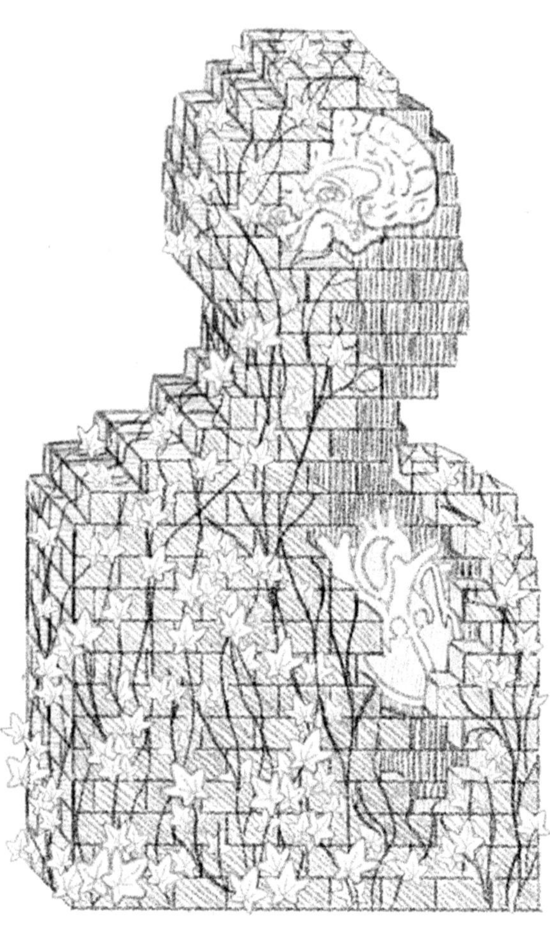

"The ivy is creeping"

The ivy is creeping
up the walls
I built around
my tender heart and
willful mind.

"only dreams can haunt me"

Vacant eyes and
dreary skies follow
the paths laid bare.

The seagulls cry
near the shores edge
as rough waves pound the sand.

It's much too late
to let past mistakes
surface once again.

So I close my book
and go upstairs where
only dreams can haunt me.

"Untitled No. 2"

Candlelit hallways of
forgotten memories
house the echoes
of ghouls I wish to meet.

In those forgotten spaces
I find the intrigue
of my soul
and its shadowed places.

The eerie calm
of those ghostly halls
settles over me in
a cloak of midnight.

If I am not careful,
this fragile hold of reality
will shatter and
I will be lost.

"my problem"

I want
to know
and yet
I do not.

And that is my problem.

"The idle lighthouse"

Take me to the idle lighthouse
that is home to doors
that transport and
leave gods and men speechless.

Faerie dust lines the nooks
and fills the cracks.
It illuminates the whispering
echoes of worlds unknown.

Lead me up the winding stair
and hand me my glinting dagger.
In the light of the moon,
steal me away to adventure.

"What adventure"

As the light filters
through leaves of golden fire,
I find my gaze
wandering the sturdy trunks.

What adventure lies
beyond that tree line?

"The cliffs are calling"

The cliffs are calling
and I'm sorry, dear,
but I must go.

To the hills, the moors.
In search of island lore.

I'm joining the fae folk,
and finding my magic.
Don't come looking;
I am no more what I once was.

"she will become"

Along the blanket sea
a path winds
and shifts by
the trumpet cliffs.

A girl is walking
toward the call of
the siren song.

She is no longer afraid,
for when she reaches those
murky depths, she will become
Fear itself.

"nothing"

Uncertainty cakes the bricks
I have used to build a wall
around my tender heart.

In fact, uncertainty is my only certainty.

I know nothing.

"Don't miss it"

Garden paths
where faeries walk
feel familiar and
yet—
not.

The glowing lights
of fireflies
flicker
and announce
a world
beyond our eyes.

Stop, listen.
The music of
the night is
the echo of
the revels they have.

Don't miss it.

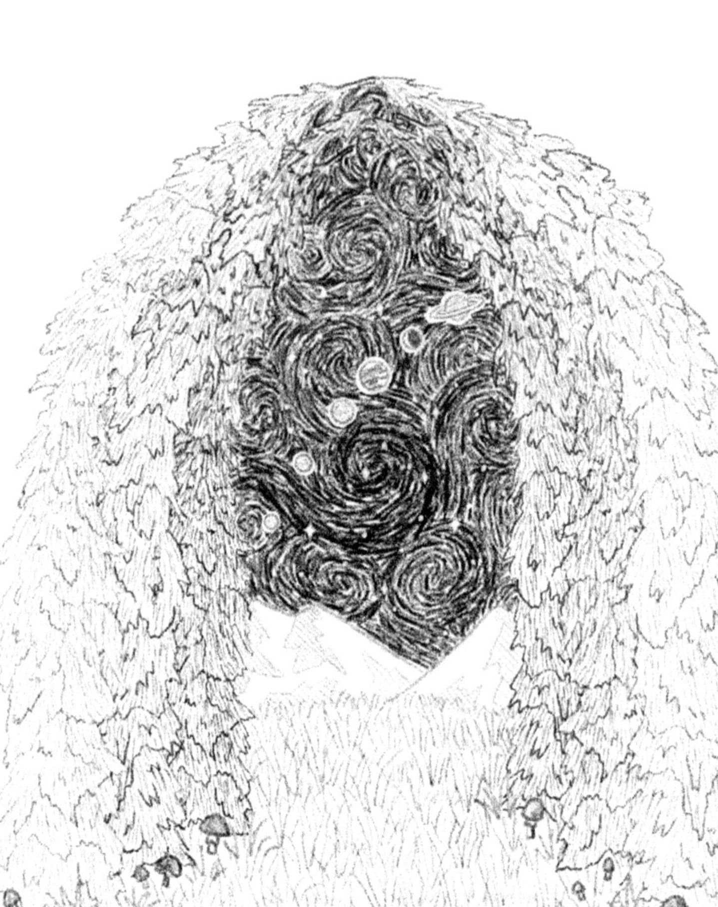

"the witching hour"

The forest comes alive
during the witching hour
or so they say.

That's when deals are struck
between worlds aligning—

But that's a story for another time.

"Beware"

The faeries are singing
in their lackadaisical way
of the bargains they'll make,
the lives they'll change
and the prisoners they shall make.

Masters of trickery
they cannot lie
yet in their eyes
are secrets kept and
deceits unshed.

Beware the faerie invitation;
the hospitality of the fae folk.
For few have returned
from their dancing rings
and those that do are changed.

"The undoing"

Untouched eyes
of dreaming hearts.

Starstruck thoughts
shoot through minds
made of fog and drear.

The undoing
is beginning again.

"mad a little while"

I wish
to go mad.
I want
to be feral
for a little while.
Nothing but
the trees
to cage me,
stars to be
my guide
and
rivers my
music.
Let me be
a nymph
and be one
with the moss
and fae folk.
Let me be
mad a little while.

"ready to be destroyed"

My mind has been turned
by the doors of the idle lighthouse.
Like a book, they take me
to faraway places.
Their adventure is my Achilles heel
and I am ready to be destroyed.

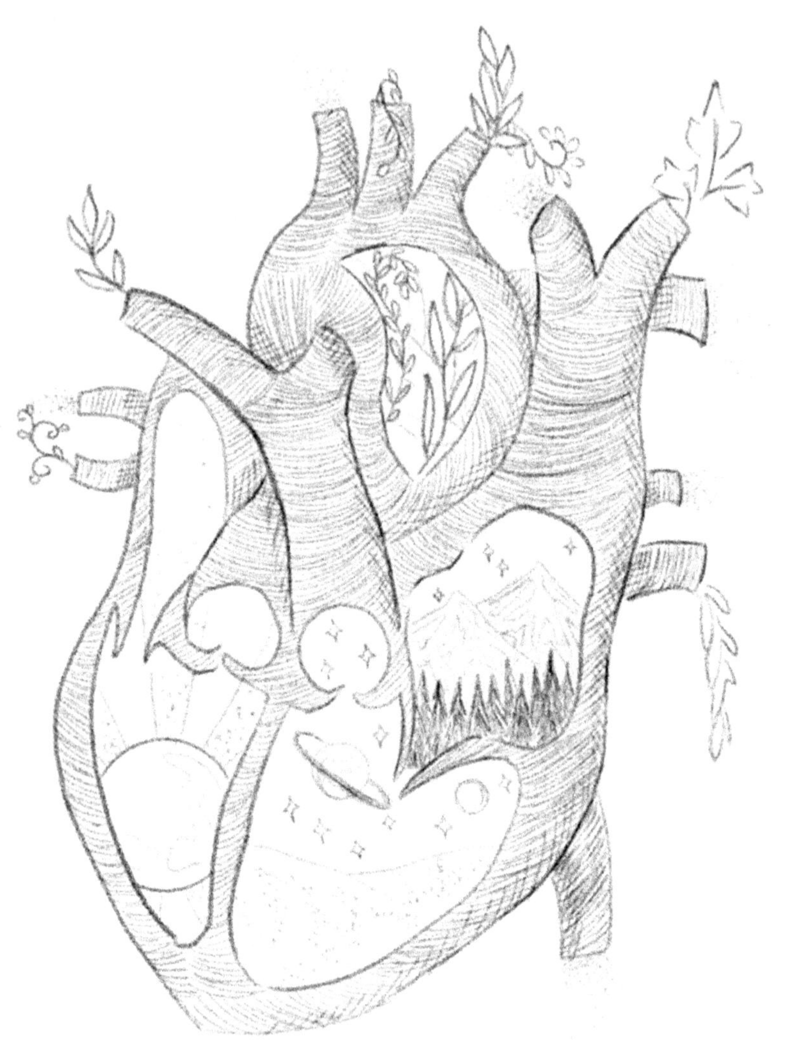

"yearning"

Incomparable yearning for
worlds unknown and
lands untraversed fills
my soular being.

What heartbreak it is
to only have one life
and find it is small
yet the world big.

"under the Artemis glow"

Sunset's molten clouds
reflect dreams left
for another day and
plans fractured from
unravelling hopes.

The last rays of daylight
make way
for moonbeams and secrets;
the idle dancing of stars
in their orbital song.

The waves push and pull
under the Artemis glow.
Oceans meet and spill
stories and tides
and mingled souls.

"I wish"

Willow leaves and
whispered dreams keep
me up and restless tonight.

Echoes heard of
sights unsought gently
prod my stagnant form.

The space between stars,
that yawning gap,
trails a finger down my spine.

Idyllic knolls of grass,
the ebb and flow of Breeze,
encompass my soul.

I wish to be anywhere.

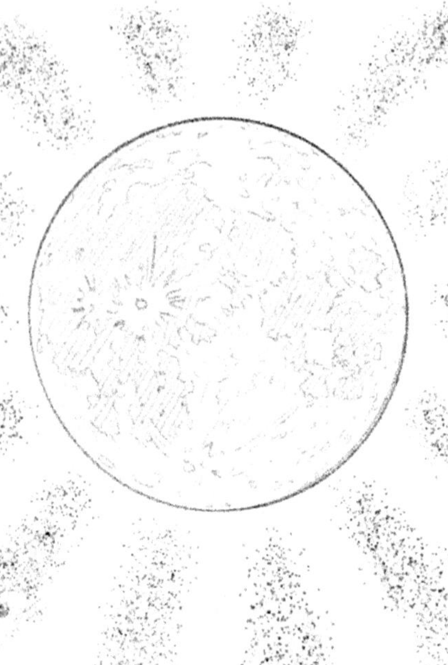

"Moonlit thoughts"

Moonlit thoughts enter
unbidden into gray matter.
They flit and twirl,
beckoning to be chased.

They wish to be pursued.

"We are returning"

The idle light of stars
shines its whimsies and musings;
entrancing all who gaze
into the glittering night.

The song between trees
cause faerie hearts to dance
and twine through misty mornings
brittle hold on magic.

And the sea foam
caresses the ocean sprites soul,
drawing it nearer to its
murky depths.

We are returning.

"the lone fisherman"

The glow of twilight hugs
the melancholy lines of
the lone fisherman.

He casts his nets
and catches dreams.

Some are small and
tossed back
into the midnight ocean.

Some he keeps;
the fat and well-lived ones.

As the dream fisherman
completes his task,
he nods to the moon.

And she smiles back.

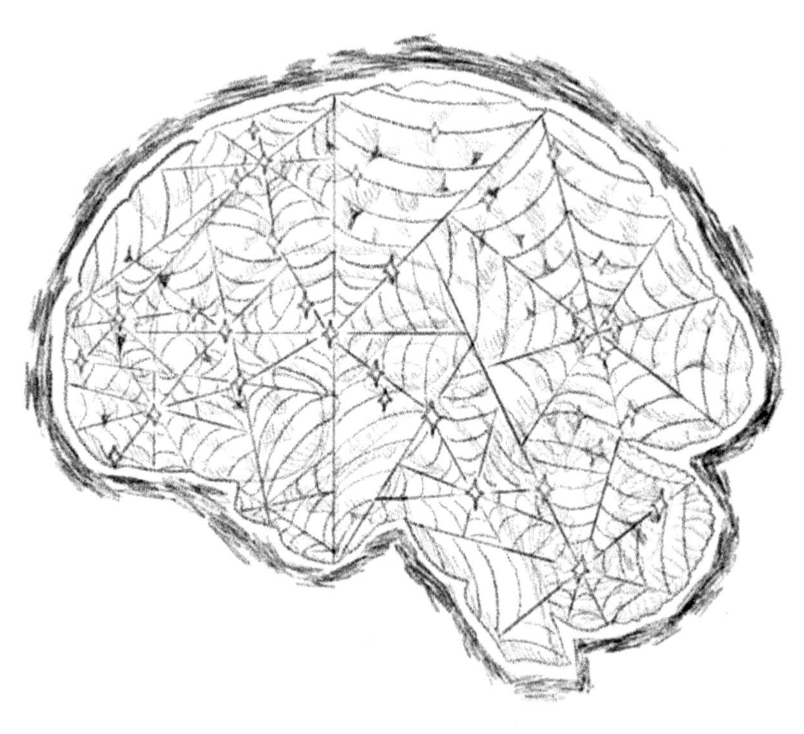

"my addlcd brain"

In the cobwebs of my addled brain
resides dewdrops of
crystalline dreams woven
with starlight threads
that glisten with
echoed longing.

"let me be"

Madness eats away at
the corners of being
trapped and caged in physicality.
It is not enough.

Oh to be the space between stars.
To distance those celestial bodies.
Let me go and
let me be.

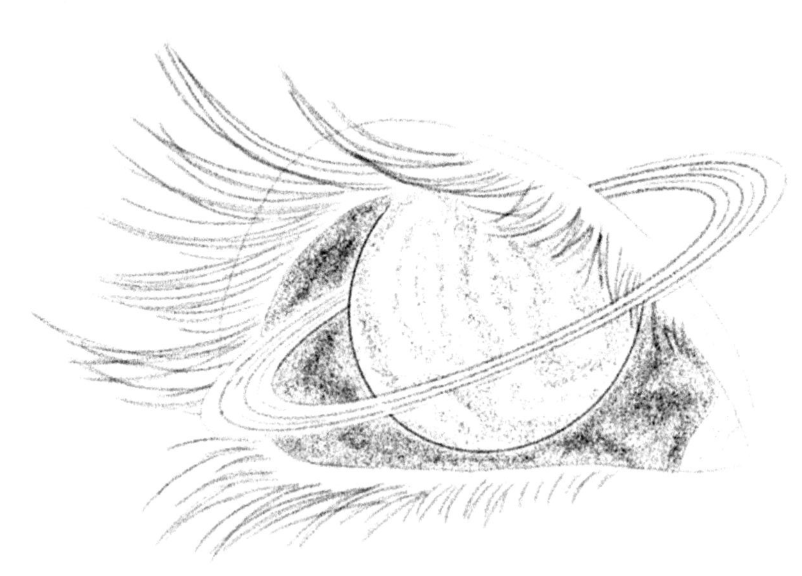

"I shall leave"

It's the closeness that concerns me.
The proximity of those dreams.
They flit into my sleep as quiet
as a feather fallen from a dove.

They stir up trouble.
For if I look at them too long,
if I listen to the murmurs,
I fear I shall leave.

And never return.

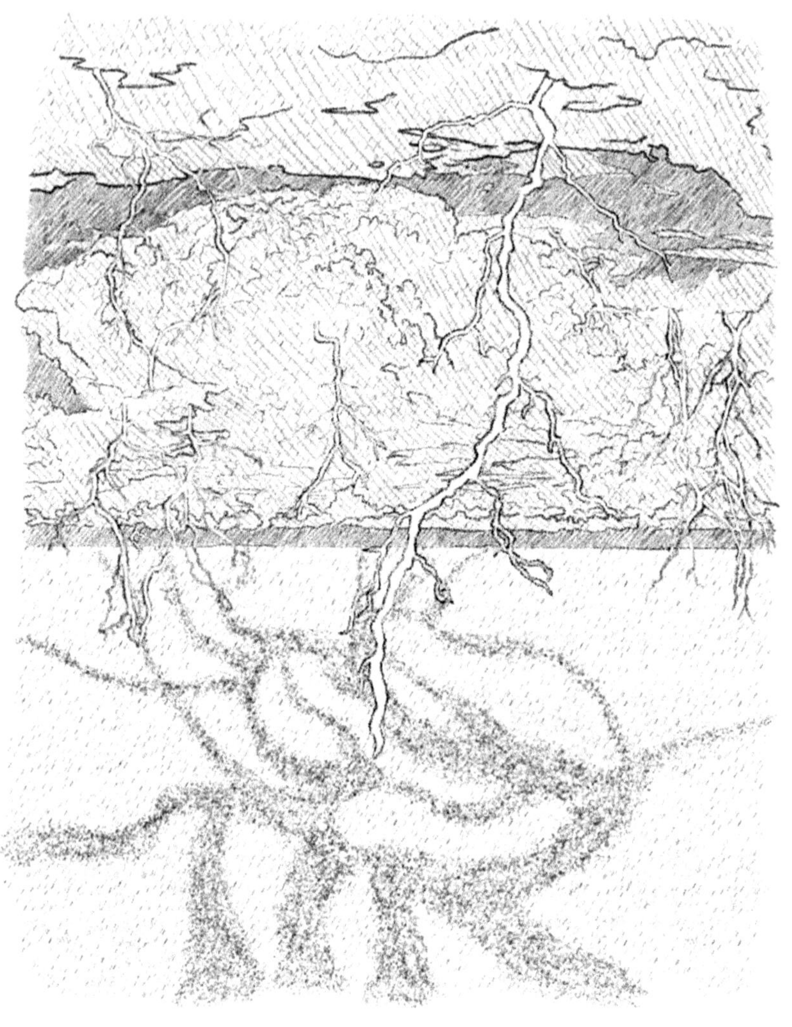

"Untitled No. 1"

Flashes of lightning
illuminate the wanderings
of my curious heart.

The rain melts and
disguises the tears of
my joy and sorrow

And as the storm rages,
so does the perseverance
of my weary and stubborn soul.

"Dragons"

In every person
there is a dragon.

My dragon likes to
warm itself in the
embers of home and
tranquility of peace.

But make no mistake—
my dragon is capable
of both tenderness and
destruction.

It can, and will,
raze villages.

Because it is still,
after all,
a dragon.

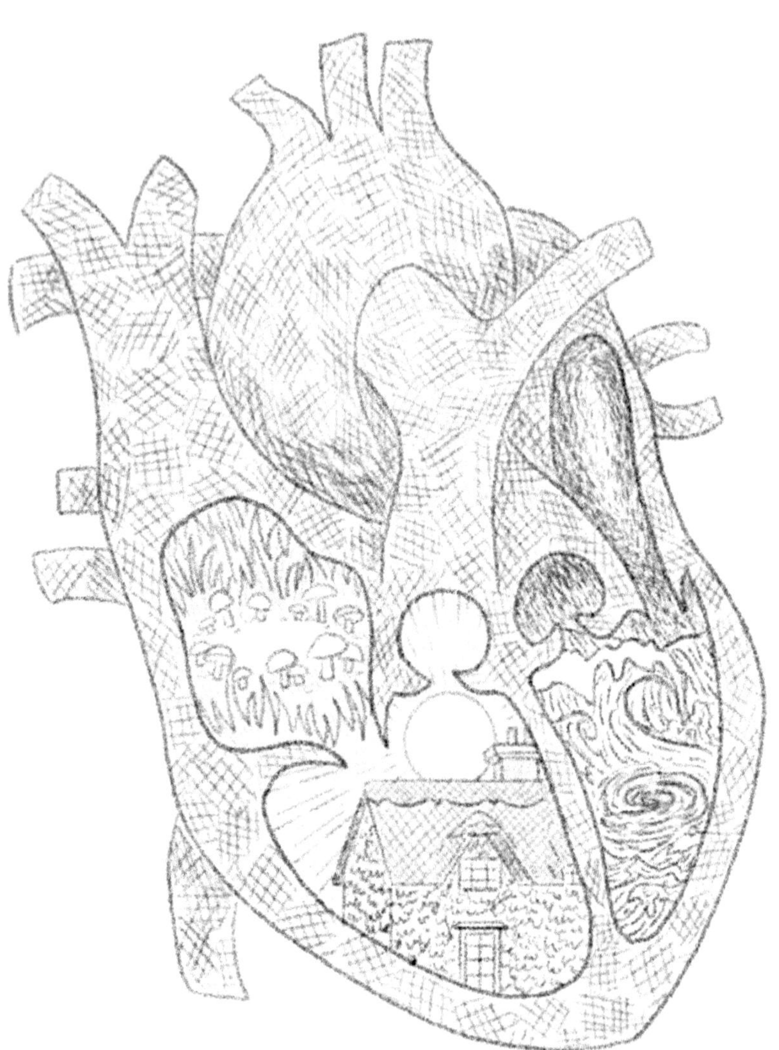

"My heart"

If you crack open the
chambers of my heart
you may be surprised to
find not a sight of
blood nor an ounce of flesh.

In one chamber there
will be a cottage;
overgrown with ivy,
it's thatched roof
warmed by my inner sun.

Another chamber houses
a faerie ring in moss.
It's ethereal glow
shines like the
laughter in my eyes.

The third has only
a vast ocean inside.
The tumultuous waves
are too strong for
even the most skilled sailor.

And the fourth chamber
is a mystery to even me.
It is dark, but not gloomy.
Peaceful and tranquil
and totally unknown.

"Human"

Anything is possible in Autumn.
It is, after all, the season of my
soul.
And winter has its merits.
But that shifting—
from warmth and color to
a glittering crystalline cold—
It is what brings my soul back
and binds it to the earth.

I am just human.

"Kiss me then"

When the air is crisp
and the night swells
to meet its midnight hour.

When the snow, thick and steady,
drifts to earth in a
confession to gravity

Kiss me then.

"cozy little heart"

In a hole in the ground
lives my stubborn little heart.
It beats and it pulses to
a steady, neat rhythm.

My heart is quite comfortable
in its round little house.
The storms and the gales
do not bother its tempo.

It is my soul that
irks and pesters my heart
and therein lies the trouble
of my cozy little heart.

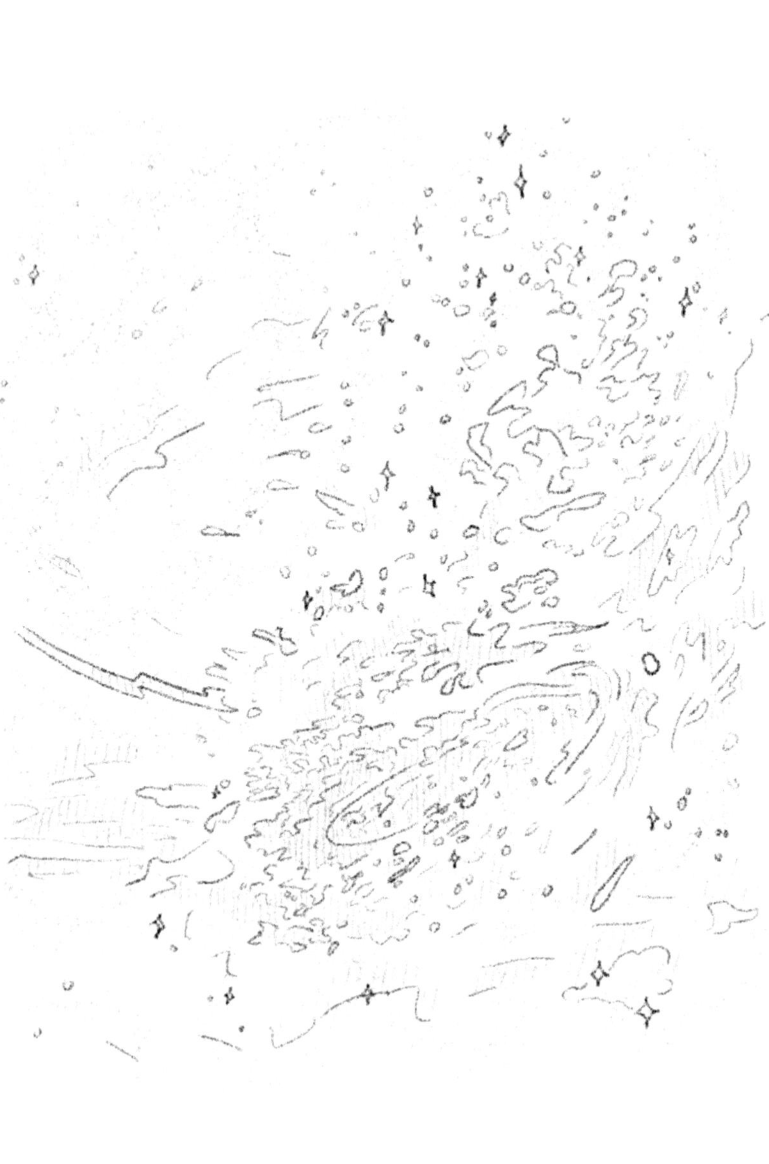

"Stars"

The stars talk at night.
They whisper secrets and stories,
things ancient and cracked.
Their twinkling voices
echo through the galaxy.

I wish to know
what the stars say
about me and my life.
I wish to hear
the secrets they keep
and the tales they tell.

Journey with me
to the stars hideaway
and maybe
one day
we will know what they keep.

"towards destiny"

In the fog
of a Darcy dawn,
you will find me
treading over the dew soaked grass.

As birds sing into
the stillness of daybreak
I hum a tune of no renown
and walk towards destiny.

"Misc."

Seaside scrapes
Seaweed cakes
My heart is an ocean away.

Lantern skies
Light goodbyes
Glance my way again.

Fluttering wings
Frightful schemes
Don't fly too close to me.

Hopeless hearts
Hurts and scars
Dancing in Paris tonight.

Rapid pulse
Roaming eyes
Steal my breath away.

Jokes on you
Jester and fool
You're magic through and through.

"Magic"

Do not dismiss
the faerie tales of old.
And do not set aside
your curiosity and wonder.

Magic is real.

Magic is you.

Acknowledgements

I always hate acknowledgements. Not only because I feel like I can't adequately say how much each person means to me, but also because there is a part of me that knows that I can't thank every single person that has helped me to get here. So, I will try my best, but just know that if you know me, you probably helped play a role in my getting to a place where I could share my work.

Thank you, obviously, to my mom and dad, whom I could not have gotten this far in life without.

Thank you to my best friend, Rhiannon. I told you I would do this, and you held me accountable to my word. You were there during turbulent times and I will never stop being grateful for your friendship.

Thank you to my dear friend Megan, who was the first to read my poems and validate my creativity. Without you these would probably still be hidden away in my notebook.

Thank you to Joanna, for helping proofread these and helping me organize them into something relatively cohesive compared to the scattered compilation that it was. And for being a great friend.

Thank you to Carys, who illustrated these words that were simply strung together. You made them come to life. Words cannot express how deeply seen I felt when I saw your illustrations of these poems.

And above all, I give my gratitude to the One who saved my soul. You are my True lighthouse.

About the Author

Karalyn works as a graphic designer and social media manager. She has a BA in Literature from Clarks Summit University. Karalyn lives in NEPA with her mountains of books and dreams of one day running away to a small cottage by the sea. The Idle Lighthouse is her first collection of poetry.

You can contact her at:
karalynelysepoetry@gmail.com.

About the Illustrator

Carys is somehow an accountant with a Bachelors of Science in counseling from Clarks Summit University. She lives in NEPA with a completely reasonable amount of plants. Carys has always loved drawing and imagining about other worlds. This is her first published collection of illustrations.

www.ingramcontent.com/pod-product-compliance
Lightning Source LLC
Chambersburg PA
CBHW070006180726
48002CB00019B/2445